the FORGOTTEN GOD

THE TRUTH ABOUT THE THIRD PERSON OF THE TRINITY

FOR TEENS · **STUDY GUIDE INCLUDED!**

CYRIL OPOKU

Book Title: *The Forgotten God: The Truth About the Third Person of the Trinity*
Author: Cyril Opoku
Cover & Interior Design by: Quest Publications
Published by: Quest Publications
ISBN: 978-1-988439-52-5
First Edition, 2025

For more information, contact:
TeenCompass Collective (www.teencompasscollective.org)
Printed in the United States of America

Contents

Preface

When I first began writing *The Forgotten God: The Truth About the Third Person of the Trinity*, I wasn't setting out to write a theological manual or a textbook on the Holy Spirit. I was writing from a place of hunger—hunger for more of God, and more specifically, a deeper relationship with the Holy Spirit.

And I realized I wasn't alone.

Over and over, I met Christians—faithful, sincere, devoted people—who loved Jesus and followed God, but rarely spoke of the Holy Spirit. Some were unsure of what to believe. Others were afraid of being "too charismatic." Still others simply hadn't been taught much about Him at all. It was as if the Spirit had become a footnote in our faith—*important*, yes, but quietly tucked away.

But the Bible paints a very different picture. The Holy Spirit is not optional. He is not confusing. He is not a backup plan. He is *God's presence in us*—the very power that raised Christ from the dead, now living within every believer. He's not meant to be forgotten. He's meant to be known, welcomed, and experienced.

This book is my invitation—to you, and to anyone who's ever wondered, *Is there more?* Yes. There is more. So much more. The Spirit of God is alive, active, and ready to move in your life in ways that are both supernatural and deeply personal.

Whether you're exploring this topic for the first time or reigniting a relationship with the Holy Spirit you've drifted from, my hope is that this book opens your heart, stretches your understanding, and most of all, draws you closer to God. Not in theory. But in daily, Spirit-empowered reality.

Let's rediscover the One we've forgotten—and invite Him to do what only He can do.

With expectation and gratitude,

Cyril O.

June 8th, 2025 (Pentecost Sunday)

Introduction

UNLEASHING THE FORGOTTEN GOD

Have you ever sensed that something essential is missing in your spiritual life—something powerful, present, yet strangely misunderstood or overlooked? For many believers, both new and seasoned, the Holy Spirit is exactly that: *the forgotten God.* This book seeks to change that, offering a clear and transformative understanding of who the Holy Spirit is and why His presence is absolutely vital in the life of every Christian.

Far too often, the Holy Spirit is reduced to vague notions—a "force," "energy," or spiritual "vibe." But the Holy Spirit is not an "it." He is a *He*— a divine Person, the third Person of the Trinity, fully God, equal in power, purpose, and glory with God the Father and God the Son. Scripture reveals that the Holy Spirit has a *mind* that understands and intercedes according to God's will, a *will* that distributes spiritual gifts as He chooses, and *emotions*—He can be grieved, and He deeply cares about how we live.

This truth isn't just theological—it's life-changing. Recognizing the Holy Spirit as a real person invites you into a relationship that will transform your everyday life. He is not an optional "bonus" in the Christian life; He is *central* to God's plan. Through Him, God actively works in the world— *and through you.*

In the chapters ahead, you'll explore who the Holy Spirit is and what He truly does. He empowers you with *supernatural strength* for living a faithful life, not through your own effort but by His presence within you. He is your *internal guide*, leading you with wisdom, peace, and purpose. As your *personal teacher*, He helps Scripture come alive, giving insight and application for your everyday choices. When you go off course, He brings *loving correction*—not to condemn, but to refine and draw you closer to Jesus.

You'll also learn how the Spirit produces the *fruit of the Spirit*—love, joy, peace, patience, and more—not through striving, but as the natural result of His work within you. You'll explore the *gifts of the Spirit*—powerful abilities God gives to His people for building up the Church and impacting the world. We'll also look at whether these gifts are still active today, and how to understand the debate around cessationism.

This book also unpacks the *baptism of the Holy Spirit*, a powerful experience available to every believer. We'll explore what it means to live a life fully yielded to the Spirit's power and how He becomes your *prayer partner*, helping you connect with God even when words fail. The Holy Spirit also plays a key role in helping you discover God's unique plan for your life— reminding you that you're never walking alone.

The core message of *The Forgotten God* is this: **You are not alone.** The Holy Spirit is your constant companion—always present, always active, always working in and through you for God's glory and your good. This book is an invitation to rediscover the person of the Holy Spirit, to embrace His presence, respond to His voice, and live a life fully empowered by Him.

So turn the page. Get ready to rediscover the Spirit you may have overlooked. You're about to encounter the One who empowers, guides, comforts, convicts, and transforms. The journey starts now—chapter one awaits.

Chapter 1

MEET THE FORGOTTEN GOD

Ever feel like there's a super important person in your life you just... don't know very well? Maybe you've heard their name, seen them around, but you haven't really connected. Sometimes, in our faith, it can feel that way with the Holy Spirit. He's often "the forgotten God". And whether you're just starting to explore faith or you've been a Christian for a while, the Holy Spirit can seem a bit mysterious, right?

You might hear people talk about the Holy Spirit as a "force" or "energy". Like some kind of spiritual electricity, or "the Force" from Star Wars – "May the Force be with you". Or maybe even just "good vibes". But here's the thing we need to lay down right from the start: the Holy Spirit is not an "it."

The Holy Spirit is a "He."

He's not just some random power floating around. The Holy Spirit is a Person. No, He doesn't have flesh and bones like we do, but He is a divine Person. He is the third Person of the Trinity, fully God, and equal to God the Father and God the Son. That's a pretty huge deal!

More Than Just a Feeling: He Thinks, Chooses, and Feels

So, if He's not just an energy or a force, what does the Bible actually tell us about who the Holy Spirit is? Great question! The Bible clearly shows us that the Holy Spirit has:

1. **A Mind:** Think about this: Romans 8:27 tells us, "The Spirit intercedes for God's people in accordance with the will of God". "Interceding" means understanding what God wants and then speaking to God on behalf of others. That's way more than some random power at work! This shows He has intelligence, understanding, and purpose. He's not just acting randomly; He's actively involved in God's plan and knows what God wants.

2. **A Will:** In 1 Corinthians 12:11, the Bible talks about how God gives different spiritual gifts to people, and it says the Spirit gives them to each one "just as he determines". The word "determines" is key here! It means making a choice, having a purpose. A basic force doesn't decide who gets what; it just *is*. But this verse clearly shows that the Spirit has His own will and acts intentionally.

3. **Emotions:** This one really blew my mind. Ephesians 4:30 says, "Do not grieve the Holy Spirit of God." Think about that for a second. Can you grieve electricity? Can you hurt the feelings of a "good vibe"? Not really. Grief is a deeply personal emotion. You can only grieve someone you have a relationship with, someone whose feelings matter to you. This verse tells us that the Holy Spirit cares deeply, and our actions can actually affect Him emotionally. It points to a real, personal connection between us and the Spirit.

So, the Bible shows us the Holy Spirit has these personal qualities: a mind, a will, and emotions. This leads us to understand the Trinity.

The Trinity: One God, Three Persons

The word "Trinity" might sound like a big, complicated theological term, but it's really at the core of who God is and where the Holy Spirit fits in. The main idea is this: Christians believe in one God. Not three separate gods, but one. However, this one God exists eternally as three distinct persons: God the Father, God the Son (Jesus), and God the Holy Spirit. They aren't just three different versions of God. It's more like three different ways that the one God is, all at the same time.

We see hints of this throughout the Bible. In Matthew 28:19, Jesus tells His followers to baptize people "in the name of the Father and of the Son and of the Holy Spirit". Notice how it says "in the name" (singular), even though He lists three persons. This points to the unity of God while still recognizing the Father, Son, and Holy Spirit as distinct individuals within that one God. It's a beautiful picture of unity and diversity.

Also, in John 14:16-17, Jesus says He's going to ask the Father to send "another advocate," the Holy Spirit, to be with us forever. The word "another" is really important here. Jesus, the Son, is one advocate (someone who stands by us). He promises to send *another* advocate, the Holy Spirit. This means the Holy Spirit is distinct from Jesus; He's not just Jesus with a different name. He's a different person who will do a similar job of helping, comforting, and supporting believers. Jesus wasn't just promising to send a feeling; He was promising to send a person to be in relationship with us.

What the Holy Spirit Does for You

Jesus goes on to explain what the Holy Spirit will do: He will teach us everything, remind us of what Jesus said, and guide us into all truth (John 14:26, 16:13). Think about it: teaching, reminding, guiding – these all require intelligence, the ability to communicate, and a purpose. These aren't things a random force can do. This shows that the Holy Spirit gets involved in our lives in a personal and meaningful way.

Understanding that the Holy Spirit is a person, a part of the Trinity, isn't just some boring theological fact. It completely changes how we can connect with God every single day! If the Holy Spirit is a person, then we can have a personal relationship with Him. He's not just a vibe we might feel at church; He can be a daily part of our lives, a constant companion. He is with us always, living inside those who believe (John 14:17). This means we can connect with Him personally, ask for His help, and experience His friendship all the time.

Sometimes, we might think of the Holy Spirit as a "cool extra" – maybe for super religious people, but not really necessary. But Jesus said something pretty different in John 16:7: "It is actually better for him to leave, so that the Spirit could come."

That's a massive statement! It shows just how vital the Holy Spirit is to God's plan. Jesus knew that the Spirit living inside believers would give them power in ways that Jesus being physically present on earth couldn't. Jesus could only be in one place at a time, but the Holy Spirit can be everywhere, in all believers, at the same time. So, the Holy Spirit is how God is actively working in the world today, through everyone who believes.

Think about all the things the Holy Spirit does in a believer's life; it's truly mind-blowing:

1. **He helps us see when we've messed up**, convicting us of sin (John 16:8). This leads us to turn away from sin and toward God.

2. **He teaches us and reminds us** of what God says is true, bringing to mind the words of Jesus (John 14:26).

3. **He gives us strength** to live for God even when it's hard, and promises us power to tell others about Jesus (Acts 1:8).

4. **He helps us to pray** even when we don't know what to say, speaking to God for us (Romans 8:26).

5. **He changes us from the inside out,** helping us become more like Jesus by producing the "fruit of the Spirit" in our lives – things like love, joy, peace, patience, kindness, goodness, faithfulness, gentleness, and self-control (Galatians 5:22-23). These aren't things we just force ourselves to do; they happen when the Holy Spirit is at work in us.

He's not just watching from the sidelines; He's in the game with us. He's the power behind our spiritual growth.

Why Do We Forget Him?

So, if He's so incredible, why might we sometimes forget about the Holy Spirit in our everyday lives?

1. **He points us to Jesus.** One big reason is that the Holy Spirit doesn't bring attention to Himself (John 16:14). His main goal is to show us who Jesus is and what He's done. So, He often works quietly, without drawing a lot of attention, making it easy to focus on other, more "obvious" parts of God.

2. **It can feel a little weird.** Talking about the Holy Spirit can sometimes feel a bit uncomfortable. We might worry about saying the wrong thing or not fully understanding Him.

3. **We like to be in control.** If we're honest, we often like to be the ones making the decisions. Letting the Holy Spirit lead can feel a little unpredictable. Following Him means trusting Him and being willing to go in directions we might not have planned. It can feel a little scary to surrender control.

But here's the truth: forgetting about the Holy Spirit means we're missing out on a close friend and a really powerful helper who is always there for us.

Your Daily Companion

Let's quickly summarize the most important things to remember about who the Holy Spirit is:

1. **The Holy Spirit is God.** He is just as much God as the Father and the Son are. He is fully God.

2. **He is a person.** This means you can have a real, everyday relationship with Him. He's not just an idea; He's a living presence in your life.

3. **He is powerful.** And His power isn't just for big miracles; it's for changing your heart and giving you the ability to live in a way that honors God.

Here's the most amazing part: If you put your trust in Jesus, the Holy Spirit actually lives inside of you! That means you are never truly alone. You always have God's power available to you, and you're never stuck relying on your own strength. You literally have God living within you. The Holy Spirit living in us is God's promise that He loves us and is actively working in our lives.

Your Challenge

Now, for a challenge to help you connect with the Holy Spirit more intentionally this week:

1. Make it a habit every day to ask the Holy Spirit to guide you, lead you, and teach you. Just invite Him into your day.

2. Try reading John chapters 14-16 slowly and carefully. As you read, really pay attention to what Jesus Himself says about the Holy Spirit – what He does, what He promises, what He's like.

3. Try praying this simple prayer every day: "Holy Spirit, help me to know You better today." Just open yourself up to the possibility of getting to know Him more.

As you go throughout your week, think about this: If the Holy Spirit, who is God Himself, lives inside of you, how might that change the way you deal with tough times, your friendships, and your journey with God? It's something truly worth pondering.

Study Guide 1

UNDERSTANDING THE HOLY SPIRIT

I. Who is the Holy Spirit?

- He is often "the forgotten God" in the lives of many Christians.

- Not an "it", "force," "energy," or "good vibes".

- He is a "He".

- He is a divine person, the third person of the Trinity, fully God, and equal to God the Father and God the Son.

II. Personal Qualities of the Holy Spirit

The Holy Spirit has personal qualities, demonstrating He is a person, not a force:

1. **A Mind:** He "intercedes for God's people in accordance with the will of God," showing intelligence, understanding, and purpose. (Romans 8:27)

2. **A Will:** He gives spiritual gifts "just as he determines," indicating choice and intentional action. (1 Corinthians 12:11)

3. **Emotions:** "Do not grieve the Holy Spirit of God" shows He can be affected emotionally, pointing to a real, personal connection. (Ephesians 4:30)

III. The Trinity

- **One God, Three Persons:** Christians believe in one God who exists eternally as three distinct persons: God the Father, God the Son (Jesus), and God the Holy Spirit.

- They are distinct individuals in one unified Godhead.

- Jesus refers to the Holy Spirit as "Another advocate," distinct from Himself but doing a similar job of helping and supporting believers. (John 14:16-17)

IV. What the Holy Spirit Does for You

The Holy Spirit is vital to God's plan and actively involved in believers' lives:

1. **Teaches, Reminds, Guides:** He teaches everything, reminds us of Jesus's words, and guides us into all truth. (John 14:26, 16:13)

2. **Convicts of Sin:** Helps us see when we've "messed up," leading us to turn toward God. (John 16:8)

3. **Gives Strength and Power:** Provides strength to live for God and power to tell others about Jesus. (Acts 1:8)

4. **Helps Us to Pray:** He intercedes for us even when we don't know what to say, speaking to God on our behalf. (Romans 8:26)

5. **Changes Us from the Inside Out:** Produces the "fruit of the Spirit" (love, joy, peace, patience, kindness, goodness, faithfulness, gentleness, and self-control), leading to transformation. (Galatians 5:22-23)

6. **Daily Companion:** He lives inside those who believe (John 14:17), making Him a constant presence and allowing for a personal relationship. It was "actually better" for Jesus to leave so the Spirit could come and be in all believers everywhere.

V. Why He Might Be "Forgotten"

1. **Points to Jesus:** The Holy Spirit doesn't bring attention to Himself; His main goal is to show us who Jesus is, often working quietly. (John 16:14)

2. **Can Feel Uncomfortable:** Talking about the Holy Spirit can sometimes feel "weird" or misunderstood.

3. **We Like Control:** Surrendering to the Holy Spirit's leading can feel unpredictable, as it means trusting Him and going in directions we might not have planned.

VI. Key Things to Remember

1. The Holy Spirit is God.

2. He is a person, enabling a real, everyday relationship.

3. He is powerful, changing our hearts and empowering us to honor God.

4. If you trust in Jesus, the Holy Spirit lives inside of you, meaning you are never alone and always have God's power available.

VII. Challenge for Deeper Connection

1. **Daily Invitation:** Ask the Holy Spirit to guide, lead, and teach you every day.

2. **Read Scripture:** Read John chapters 14-16 slowly, focusing on Jesus's words about the Holy Spirit.

3. **Simple Prayer:** Pray daily, "Holy Spirit, help me to know You better today."

Chapter 2

WHAT DOES THE HOLY SPIRIT DO?

When you hear the words "Holy Spirit," what comes to mind? For a lot of people, the image is fuzzy—something like a mysterious force or a vague spiritual vibe. It can feel hard to define, especially if no one has ever really explained it clearly. But here's the truth: the Holy Spirit isn't a vague energy or distant concept. He's a person—the third person of the Trinity. He's God, and He's with us.

That's not just a theological idea—it's a life-changing reality. Understanding who the Holy Spirit is helps us understand what He does, and why it matters for your everyday life. As a teenager trying to follow Jesus, this matters more than you might realize.

So, let's get into it. What does the Holy Spirit actually do—and how can His presence shape the way you live, choose, love, and grow every day?

1. Empowerment: More Than Just Willpower

Living out the Christian life, truly living it, can be incredibly tough sometimes, right? Think about it:

1. Being kind when you absolutely do not feel like it.
2. Standing up for what's right when everyone else around you is going the other way.
3. Truly loving people, even the ones who are difficult.

These things take something extra. They definitely take more than just gritting your teeth and relying on your own willpower. And that's exactly where the Holy Spirit steps in. He provides that supernatural boost you can't conjure up on your own.

Remember what Jesus told His followers in Acts 1:8? He said, "But you will receive power when the Holy Spirit has come upon you and you will be my witnesses". This isn't just about sharing your faith; it's about being able to live a life that reflects Jesus, in every place and every situation.

Now, are we talking about literal superpowers or miracles? Well, sometimes maybe, but that's not the primary way the Holy Spirit empowers us for daily life. Mostly, it's about an inner power, a deep-seated strength for everyday stuff. Think of it as an internal engine, giving you the spiritual horsepower to honor God in all you do.

For example, imagine you're at school, and you feel a knot in your stomach when the conversation turns to faith. You want to share what you believe, but nervousness washes over you. The Holy Spirit can step in and give you that courage, that unexpected boldness to speak up, even when your voice feels shaky. Or maybe you're facing a choice – one way is easy and popular, but you know deep down it's wrong. The Holy Spirit gives you the strength to do the right thing anyway, even when it means going against the current. It's an inner boost when you need it, especially with all the pressures you face as teenagers. This empowerment gives you boldness and conviction, enabling you to navigate those challenging moments with integrity.

2. Guidance: Your Internal GPS

Life is full of choices, and for teens, it can feel overwhelmingly complex. You're trying to figure out friendships, school drama, what to do after graduation, and navigating relationships, all while trying to figure out who *you* are. Which way do you go when there are so many paths and voices pulling you in different directions?

This is where the Holy Spirit acts as an internal guide. Jesus promised this, saying in John 16:13, "When the Spirit of truth comes, he will guide you into all the truth". It's like having a personal mentor living inside you, constantly helping you align your choices and your path with God's overarching plan for your life.

So, what does this guidance actually feel like? It's not usually a booming voice from the sky. Sometimes, it might manifest as a strong sense of peace about a decision. You just "know deep down it's right," a quiet assurance settling over you. Other times, it's more like a "check in your spirit," a subtle feeling that something's off. It's a gentle nudge, perhaps steering you away from a choice that might lead you astray.

Learning to listen for this guidance takes practice, but it's incredibly valuable. It's often that "still small voice," an inner sense of direction, rather than a loud, obvious command. Imagine you're trying to decide whether to join a certain group or activity. You might feel a sense of unease, a quiet warning sign, even if it looks good on the surface. That's the Holy Spirit's gentle nudge, guiding you away from something that isn't quite right for you, or isn't in line with God's best. This internal compass helps you navigate the confusing map of life, pointing you towards truth and wisdom.

3. Teaching: Unlocking God's Word

Have you ever been reading the Bible, perhaps a part you've read countless times before, and suddenly, *bang*, it just clicks? You see something you never noticed, a truth you never grasped, and it feels like a lightbulb just went off? Those "aha moments" are truly amazing, aren't they?

Well, that's often the Holy Spirit at work. He is our personal teacher. Jesus promised this very thing in John 14:26: "But the Helper, the Holy Spirit, whom the Father will send in my name, he will teach you all things and bring to your remembrance all that I have said to you".

This means the Spirit doesn't just help you read words on a page; He helps you actually understand the Bible. He illuminates its truths, helping you grasp profound spiritual concepts that might otherwise seem confusing. And it's not just about understanding; He helps you remember it when you need it most, bringing to mind a specific verse or principle exactly when you're facing a challenge or a tough decision. Crucially, He helps you figure out how to live it out in your daily life. He's like a personal tutor for God's word, making it relevant and applicable to your unique experiences as a teen. This makes studying the Bible an active, transformative experience, not just a chore.

4. Conviction: Loving Correction

The word "conviction" can sound a bit heavy, right? It might make you think of feeling guilty, ashamed, or like you're being harshly judged. But when we talk about the Holy Spirit's conviction, it's actually incredibly loving. It's not about shaming us or beating us down.

Instead, conviction is about the Holy Spirit helping us see where we've gone wrong. His goal isn't to condemn you, but to highlight areas in your life so you can grow and become more like Jesus. It's correction, but born out of deep, unconditional love.

Jesus Himself mentioned this in John 16:8, stating that the Spirit would come to "convict the world concerning sin and righteousness and judgment". For us, this often feels like a gentle nudge. It's that quiet voice in your mind saying, "Hey, maybe rethink that decision you just made," or "This isn't quite right, is it?". It's a loving course correction, pointing out where you might have missed the mark and encouraging you to turn back to God. It's not harsh judgment, but rather a supportive guide inviting you back to the right path.

Imagine you said something mean about a friend behind their back, and later, you feel a lingering unease, a sense of "that wasn't okay." That's the Holy Spirit's loving conviction at work. He's not shaming you; He's simply pointing out the misstep, prompting you to apologize, make amends, and choose kindness next time. It's an invitation back to alignment with God's character and your best self. This transformative aspect helps you learn and mature in your faith.

5. Fruit of the Spirit: Growing Goodness

Linked to this process of growth and conviction is something really positive: the fruit of the Spirit. You've probably heard of them: "love, joy, peace, forbearance, kindness, goodness, faithfulness, gentleness, and self-control". These are the qualities described in Galatians 5:22-23.

Here's the thing about this fruit: they're not things you just try harder to be. While we certainly cooperate with God, these qualities primarily grow in us because the Holy Spirit is living in us. They are the natural, beautiful result of His presence within you.

So, as we follow Jesus and actively let the Spirit lead our lives, these qualities don't just appear magically, but they start showing up more and more. You'll find yourself actually changing, becoming more patient, more joyful, more self-controlled. This is huge, especially if you struggle with things like impatience or getting angry easily – and let's be honest, we all do at times. These fruits aren't about gritting your teeth and forcing yourself to be "nicer." Instead, it's the Spirit's power working inside you that helps them develop and flourish. Knowing this takes so much pressure off, because it highlights His role, not just your struggle. It's a reminder that you're not trying to do this alone.

For instance, if you usually react to frustrating situations with immediate anger, you might find that as you lean into the Spirit, you experience a moment of peace, allowing you to respond with gentleness or self-control instead. This is the Spirit growing His fruit within you, making you more like Jesus.

6. Gifts of the Spirit: Equipping for Service

Related to the fruit of the Spirit are the gifts of the Spirit. These aren't just your natural talents, though God certainly uses those. These are specific spiritual abilities given by the Holy Spirit. 1 Corinthians 12:4-11 talks about these, listing things like wisdom, knowledge, faith, healing, prophecy, and many other diverse gifts.

Here's an important point: everyone gets something different. The whole idea isn't for everyone to have the same gift. Instead, the Spirit gives different gifts to different people, creating a beautiful tapestry of abilities within the community of believers.

Why different ones? The ultimate purpose is to build up the church, to serve each other, and to bring glory to God. Maybe someone has a special gift for teaching, making complex truths easy for others to understand. Someone else might be amazing at encouragement, always knowing just what to say to lift people up. Others might have gifts of leadership, or helping, or discernment, or mercy. Each gift is vital and plays a crucial role in the body of Christ.

It's about using what God gives you to help others. These gifts are not for showing off or for personal gain. Each gift, no matter how seemingly big or small, is important, given by God to serve others and ultimately bring

Him glory. We all work together, like different parts of a team, contributing our unique strengths for the common good. As a teen, recognizing your spiritual gifts, even if they're still emerging, can empower you to serve your friends, family, and community in impactful ways.

You Are Not Alone

Wow. So, we've covered a lot, haven't we? We've explored the Holy Spirit's roles in empowerment, guidance, teaching, conviction, growing fruit, and giving gifts. That's an incredible list, showing just how active and involved the Holy Spirit truly is in our lives.

So, pulling it all together, what's the big message here? Why does all this matter, especially for you, our reader?

The absolute main thing, the core truth to grasp from all of this, is that you are not alone in this. Not ever. The Holy Spirit is right there with you, actively working. He is:

- Giving you strength and courage.
- Guiding your choices.
- Helping you understand God's word.
- Gently correcting you when you stumble.
- Growing good things in you, like love and peace.
- Equipping you with unique abilities to serve.

And that's huge, right? Especially when you're a teenager facing all the confusion, the pressure, the changes, the sometimes overwhelming feeling that you have to figure everything out on your own. Knowing you have the Holy Spirit inside you – that's a source of real strength, real peace, real confidence. You don't have to navigate it all by yourself. You're not expected to do this Christian life thing alone. Not at all. That was never God's plan.

The Holy Spirit is your constant companion and helper, always present, always active, always working for your good and God's glory.

As you go about your week, remember this truth: The Holy Spirit is with you. He is empowering you, guiding you, teaching you, and helping you grow. You are not alone. Lean into that. Let the Spirit lead you in every decision, every challenge, and every step of your journey. Embrace His presence, listen to His voice, and watch as He transforms you from the inside out.

Study Guide 2

THE ACTIVE WORK OF THE HOLY SPIRIT

I. Who is the Holy Spirit?

- The Holy Spirit is not a vague energy or force, but a Person—the third person of the Trinity and God Himself.

- He is with us, which is a life-changing reality.

II. What Does the Holy Spirit Do?

The Holy Spirit actively works in our lives in several key ways:

1. Empowerment: More Than Just Willpower

- Provides supernatural boost and inner power for daily Christian living.

- Gives courage and boldness to speak about faith or do the right thing, even under pressure.

- Helps with difficult actions like being kind, standing up for what's right, and loving difficult people.

- It's an internal engine for honoring God.

2. Guidance: Your Internal GPS

- Acts as an internal guide and personal mentor.

- Helps align choices with God's plan.

- Manifests as a strong sense of peace, a "check in your spirit," or a gentle nudge.

- It's a "still small voice," an inner sense of direction.

3. Teaching: Unlocking God's Word

- Is our personal teacher.

- Helps us understand the Bible, illuminates its truths, and helps us grasp profound spiritual concepts.

- Helps us remember relevant verses and apply them to daily life.

4. Conviction: Loving Correction

- Is about helping us see where we've gone wrong, not to condemn or shame us, but to help us grow.

- Feels like a gentle nudge or a quiet voice pointing out missteps.

- It's a loving course correction and an invitation back to alignment with God's character.

5. Fruit of the Spirit: Growing Goodness

- Qualities like love, joy, peace, patience, kindness, goodness, faithfulness, gentleness, and self-control.

- These qualities are the natural result of the Holy Spirit's presence within us, not just human effort.

- The Spirit's power helps them develop and flourish.

6. Gifts of the Spirit: Equipping for Service

- o These are specific spiritual abilities given by the Holy Spirit, distinct from natural talents.

- o Examples include wisdom, knowledge, faith, healing, prophecy, teaching, encouragement, leadership, helping, discernment, or mercy.

- o Different gifts are given to different people to build up the church, serve each other, and bring glory to God.

- o Each gift is vital and plays a crucial role.

III. The Core Message: You Are Not Alone

- The absolute main truth is that you are not alone; the Holy Spirit is constantly with you and actively working.

- He is your constant companion and helper, always present, always active, always working for your good and God's glory.

- Embrace His presence and let Him lead you.

Chapter 3

THE BAPTISM OF THE HOLY SPIRIT

If you've ever heard the phrase "baptism of the Holy Spirit" and felt a little unsure—or even a bit weirded out—you're not alone. It might sound like some old-school church tradition or something reserved for super-spiritual people. But what if this idea is actually something powerful, personal, and meant for every follower of Jesus?

In this chapter, we're going to unpack what the Bible really says about the baptism of the Holy Spirit. We'll look at where it shows up in Scripture, what it means, and why it still matters today. This isn't just about theology—it's about power, purpose, and living the kind of life God designed you for.

Let's dive in and explore how the Holy Spirit isn't just someone we talk about—He's someone we experience.

What Does "Baptized in the Holy Spirit" Even Mean?

Imagine you've got a super cool phone, right? You *have* the phone, it's in your pocket. That's kind of like when you first believe in Jesus – the Holy Spirit comes to live inside you. He's there. But what if that phone was super powerful, with amazing features, but it was just sitting there, not even turned on or connected to Wi-Fi? You wouldn't be using its full potential, would you?

Well, being baptized in the Holy Spirit is like totally powering up that phone. It's when the Holy Spirit comes into your life in a super powerful, personal way. It's like He's filling you up, giving you strength, empowering you to live your life boldly guided by Him. This isn't just about knowing facts about God in your head. It's way beyond just understanding Bible stories; it's about being filled with God's own power, feeling His presence with you, and tapping into the very purpose He has for your life.

Is This Even a Bible Thing?

Absolutely! This idea isn't something someone just made up. It's straight from the Bible. Check out Acts 1:8. This is Jesus talking to His followers *after* He came back to life. They already believed in Him; they'd walked with Him and knew He was the Messiah. But He told them, "you will receive power when the Holy Spirit has come upon you, and you will be my witnesses".

Think about it: they already believed, so why did they need to wait for this "power"? Because they needed a *specific kind* of power and enablement to actually do what Jesus was calling them to do – to be His witnesses effectively.

And they *did* wait! Then, we see the amazing fulfillment in Acts 2:4, during the famous event of Pentecost. It says, "And they were all filled with the Holy Spirit and began to speak in other tongues as the Spirit gave them utterance".

Think about those disciples. Before this, they were scared and hiding out after Jesus's death. But *after* Pentecost, they stepped out and boldly, publicly told everyone about Jesus. That massive shift wasn't just them trying harder; it came directly from the power of the Holy Spirit filling them. It was like their "inner superpower" was unleashed!

One-Time Experience or Ongoing Power-Ups?

This is a really common question, and honestly, Christians have different understandings about it based on the Bible.

- Some believe that the moment you first become a Christian and put your faith in Jesus, you're also baptized in the Holy Spirit. You receive Him, and you're joined to Christ's body by the Spirit. For them, it's a simultaneous experience.

- Others believe it can often be a distinct experience that happens *after* you become a believer. We see examples of this pattern in the Book of Acts:

    o In Samaria, people had believed in Jesus and were even baptized in water, but they didn't receive the Holy Spirit in this empowering way until Peter and John came and prayed for them.

    o In Ephesus, Paul met some disciples who hadn't even heard of the Holy Spirit. When he laid hands on them, the Holy Spirit came upon them.

    o And get this: In Acts 10, the Holy Spirit came on Cornelius and his whole household *while they were still listening to Peter speak*, even before they were baptized in water!

So, the Bible shows us that the timing can definitely vary. It wasn't always the exact same sequence in the early church.

What's also super interesting is that even though the Holy Spirit comes into your life when you first believe (He "indwells" every believer), the Bible also encourages us to keep being filled with the Spirit. Like in Ephesians 5:18, it suggests an ongoing experience, not just a one-and-done moment.

Think of it like this: having the Holy Spirit living inside you is like owning that powerful phone. But being baptized in the Spirit, and continually being filled, is like being fully immersed in the signal, totally powered up, constantly connected and guided by that network. It's about being fully activated by Him.

Why Should *You* Even Care?

Okay, this is the big one. Why should this even be on your radar? You should care because, honestly, you were never meant to try and live this Christian life on your own strength. It's just too hard! God knew you'd face challenges, temptations, and situations that require something way beyond what you naturally have.

Like what kind of things?

- Needing actual strength to say no to sin – those temptations that try to pull you away from God.

- Needing the courage to speak up about your faith when it feels awkward or unpopular at school or with friends.

- Needing strength when you're feeling totally weak, down, or overwhelmed by life's pressures.

- Needing wisdom to make good choices, not just guessing your way through tough decisions.

- And let's not forget that deep, real joy and unshakable peace that the Holy Spirit brings, even when things are tough.

The baptism of the Holy Spirit isn't just some abstract religious idea or an "optional extra" for super-Christians. It's about getting the actual divine power you need to live out the purpose God has specifically for *you*. You weren't just made to go through the motions of religion like checking off a to-do list. You were made for a life that's alive, dynamic, impactful, and fully powered by God's Spirit!.

Is This for Everyone? (Spoiler: YES!)

Good news! This experience, this baptism, is absolutely for everyone who decides to follow Jesus. Acts 2:38-39 makes this super clear. After Peter preaches on Pentecost, people ask what they should do. Peter tells the crowd to "Repent and be baptized... and you will receive the gift of the Holy Spirit". Then he adds this crucial part: "For the promise is for you and for your children and for all who are far off—everyone whom the Lord our God calls".

"All who are far off"? That sounds pretty inclusive, right? That promise wasn't just for the people standing there 2,000 years ago. It's explicitly for their kids and for everyone whom the Lord calls throughout history. And guess what? That includes *you* listening right now!.

What Does It Actually Feel/Look Like?

Okay, so if you experience this, what might it actually feel like? Is it always some huge, dramatic lights-flashing kind of thing?

Here's the deal: the experience can be different for everyone. It's not always this massive outward event, though sometimes it can be very powerful and tangible.

- Some people might feel strong emotions like overwhelming love or joy.

- Others might just sense a profound, deep feeling of peace and God's closeness.

- And yes, the Bible *does* mention speaking in other languages (often called "speaking in tongues") as one possible manifestation when the Holy Spirit comes upon someone powerfully, like at Pentecost. But it's not the only way the Spirit shows up, and the Bible doesn't say that *everyone* who is baptized in the Spirit will always speak in tongues. It's one possible sign, but not the definitive one for everyone.

So, if it's not always tongues or big emotions, what are some of the real signs—the "fruit"—that someone has been baptized or is being continually filled with the Holy Spirit? You should look for:

- A stronger, more passionate love for Jesus growing in you.

- A new boldness or confidence to share what you believe, even when it's scary.

- A deeper hunger than before to read and understand the Bible.

- A real, genuine desire bubbling up to help and serve other people.

- And definitely a growing sensitivity to the Holy Spirit's voice and guidance in your decisions, big and small.

These inward changes and outward actions are often the most important and lasting signs that the Spirit is actively working and empowering you.

How Do I Get This "Superpower"?

So, you're following Jesus, and you're like, "Okay, I want this! I want this deeper experience, this empowerment." What should you do? How do you receive the baptism of the Holy Spirit?

The first and most important thing is actually really simple: Ask God for it! Just ask sincerely. Jesus himself gives us this incredible encouragement in Luke 11:13. He says, "If you then, though you are evil, know how to give good gifts to your children, how much more will your Father in heaven give the Holy Spirit to those who ask him?".

Wow! "How much more"? That's pretty direct. God wants to give this gift. The invitation is right there from Jesus himself. He basically says, if you ask, the Father *loves* to give the Spirit.

So, it's really as simple as just asking God in prayer. No complicated ritual needed. You can come to God honestly, sincerely, in prayer, and specifically ask Him to baptize you, to fill you, to immerse you in the Holy Spirit.

You could even pray something simple like this: "Holy Spirit, I want everything You have for me. I really do. Please fill me, baptize me, and give me Your power so I can live boldly for Jesus. I surrender my life, my will, all of it to You right now. Lead me, use me, change me from the inside out. In Jesus' name, Amen".

The real key is coming with an open, expectant heart, genuinely ready and willing to let the Holy Spirit work in your life however He chooses, trusting that He hears you and wants to fill you.

Your Challenge: Don't Live on "Low Battery"!

As we wrap up, here's the biggest takeaway: Don't just settle for knowing *about* the Holy Spirit from a distance. Don't let Him be the forgotten God in your life.

Instead, really seek to experience Him personally. Don't try to live for God using just your own limited willpower and strength, running on "low battery" all the time. Learn what it means to live *with* God day by day, moment by moment, through the active power of His Spirit inside you.

Remember, you were made for a life of real spiritual power, God-given purpose, and His tangible presence. And that kind of life is truly made possible through the baptism and the ongoing filling of the Holy Spirit. It's His gift to empower you for everything He's called you to be and do!.

So, here's your challenge: Take a moment today and, like we talked about, simply ask God to fill you with His Holy Spirit. Come with an open heart, ready to be powered up, and see how He begins to transform your life from the inside out. You've got this!

Study Guide 3

THE BAPTISM OF THE HOLY SPIRIT UNPACKED

I. Understanding the Concept

- The "baptism of the Holy Spirit" might sound unfamiliar, but it is powerful, personal, and intended for every follower of Jesus.

- It's about experiencing the Holy Spirit actively, not just talking about Him.

- Imagine owning a powerful phone that's just sitting there; receiving the Holy Spirit when you believe in Jesus is like having the phone. Being baptized in the Holy Spirit is like "totally powering up that phone".

- It means the Holy Spirit comes into your life in a super powerful, personal way, filling you up, giving you strength, and empowering you to live boldly guided by Him. It's about being filled with God's own power and tapping into your purpose.

II. Biblical Foundation

- This concept is straight from the Bible.

- Jesus told His followers (who already believed in Him) that they would "receive power when the Holy Spirit has come upon you" to be His witnesses [Acts 1:8].

- This promise was fulfilled at Pentecost [Acts 2:4] when the disciples were "filled with the Holy Spirit and began to speak in other tongues". This event transformed them from being scared to boldly speaking about Jesus.

III. One-Time Event or Ongoing Experience?

- Christians have different understandings.

    o Some believe it happens simultaneously with salvation.
    o Others believe it can be a distinct experience after believing.

- The Book of Acts shows varied timing:

    o People in Samaria believed but received the Spirit later when prayed for [Acts 8].

    o Disciples in Ephesus hadn't heard of the Holy Spirit and received Him when Paul laid hands on them [Acts 19].

    o Cornelius and his household received the Spirit *before* water baptism [Acts 10].

- Even if the Spirit indwells every believer at conversion, the Bible also encourages continual "being filled" with the Spirit [Ephesians 5:18], suggesting an ongoing experience. It's like being continually immersed in the signal, totally powered up.

IV. Why It Matters for You

- You were never meant to live the Christian life on your own strength; it's too hard.

- Spirit baptism provides the divine power you need for:
    - Strength to say no to sin.
    - Courage to speak up about your faith.
    - Strength when you feel weak or overwhelmed.
    - Wisdom for tough decisions.
    - Deep joy and unshakable peace.

- It's not an "optional extra" but about getting the actual divine power to live out God's purpose for you, enabling a dynamic and impactful life.

V. Is It For Everyone?

- Yes, absolutely! This experience is for everyone who follows Jesus.

- Peter declared the promise of the Holy Spirit is "for you and for your children and for all who are far off—everyone whom the Lord our God calls" [Acts 2:38-39]. This includes you today.

VI. What to Expect (Feelings & Signs)

- The experience can be different for everyone; it's not always a huge, dramatic event.
    - Some may feel overwhelming love or joy.
    - Others might sense a profound peace and God's closeness.
    - Speaking in tongues is *one possible manifestation*, but not the only or definitive sign for everyone.

- Real signs that the Spirit is actively working and empowering you are:
    - A stronger, more passionate love for Jesus.

o   New boldness or confidence to share your faith.
o   A deeper hunger to read and understand the Bible.
o   A genuine desire to help and serve others.
o   A growing sensitivity to the Holy Spirit's voice and guidance.

VII. How to Receive This "Superpower"

- The first and most important step is simple: Ask God for it!
- Jesus encourages us: "How much more will your Father in heaven give the Holy Spirit to those who ask him?" [Luke 11:13].
- You can ask God sincerely in prayer to baptize or fill you with the Holy Spirit.
- Come with an open, expectant heart, ready and willing to let the Holy Spirit work however He chooses.

VIII. Challenge: Don't Live on "Low Battery"!

- Don't settle for just knowing about the Holy Spirit; seek to experience Him personally.
- Don't try to live for God using only your own willpower, running on "low battery".
- Embrace the life of real spiritual power, God-given purpose, and His tangible presence that the Holy Spirit makes possible.
- Take a moment today and simply ask God to fill you with His Holy Spirit.

Chapter 4

SUPERNATURAL YOU?
THE GIFTS OF THE SPIRIT TODAY

Have you ever felt like your faith is stuck in neutral—like it's mostly about going to church, trying to be a good person, and hoping God is listening somewhere in the distance? If so, you're not alone. And when it comes to the Holy Spirit, some of the terms you hear—like "prophecy," "speaking in tongues," or "healing"—can sound confusing, outdated, or even a little intimidating.

It's easy to assume that those spiritual gifts were only for the early church, for the apostles, or for ultra-spiritual people who seem to have everything figured out. But what if those gifts weren't just part of ancient history? What if they were meant for believers today—including you?

In this chapter, we're going to explore what the Bible actually says about the gifts of the Spirit. Are they still active? What are they for? And how can they be a part of your own walk with God right now?

Not a Cookie Cutter God: Gifts for the Common Good

Let's start with a foundational spot in the Bible: Paul's first letter to the Corinthians, chapter 12. In verses 4-7, it says:

"Now there are varieties of gifts, but the same Spirit. And there are varieties of service, but the same Lord. And there are varieties of activities, but it is the

same God who empowers them all in everyone. To each is given the manifestation of the Spirit for the common good."

There's so much packed in there! First, it says "varieties of gifts, but the same Spirit". This immediately tells us that God doesn't use a cookie cutter. There's an amazing diversity in how the Spirit works. It's not just one or two ways; it's a whole spectrum! And even though there are different expressions, they all come from the same single source: the Holy Spirit, the Lord, the same God.

Then there's that last part: "to each is given the manifestation of the Spirit for the common good". This is super important. It means these gifts aren't primarily for *your* personal spotlight or to make *you* feel super spiritual. While they definitely benefit you, their main purpose is serving others and building up the whole community of the church. Think of it like this: if someone has an amazing talent for playing guitar, they don't just play for themselves in their room; they share that gift to bless others, maybe at a school concert or a worship service. It's the same idea with spiritual gifts.

Why is understanding this so important, especially for you right now? Because it means God isn't some distant force. He actually wants to be active *through you*, right now. The Holy Spirit living inside you wants to empower you, giving you abilities to make a real difference. Your life isn't just about sitting back; it has purpose and power through Him. This changes everything about how you see your faith journey! And honestly, the church today, including your generation, desperately needs the gifts the Spirit gives. They're not optional extras; they're vital for the church to be healthy and grow.

So, What Are These Gifts, Anyway?

Okay, so we know *why* they matter and *where* they come from. But what *are* these gifts specifically? Paul lists quite a few in different places, like 1 Corinthians 12, Romans 12, and Ephesians 4. Here's a quick rundown:

- **Prophecy:** This is basically speaking truth that comes from the Spirit's prompting. It's not necessarily predicting the future, but often speaking God's heart or a message of encouragement, challenge, or comfort.

- **Speaking in Tongues:** Speaking in languages you haven't learned by the Spirit's power.

- **Interpretation of Tongues:** The ability to understand and explain what was said when someone speaks in tongues.

- **Healing:** God restoring health in supernatural ways.

- **Miracles:** Acts that go beyond natural explanation.

- **Words of Wisdom/Knowledge:** Spirit-given insight into a situation or truth that you wouldn't know naturally.

- **Discernment:** Figuring out if something—an idea, a teaching, or an action—is really from God or not.

But wait, there are also gifts like:

- Teaching
- Encouragement
- Service
- Leadership
- Giving
- Acts of Mercy

You might be thinking, "Those last ones sound a bit more ordinary, like things people just do!". That's a really good point. Some gifts definitely seem more obviously supernatural, like miracles or tongues. But here's the key: the Bible's perspective is that ALL these gifts, whether they look spectacular or practical, originate from the same Holy Spirit. So, even the gift of showing mercy, when it's empowered by the Spirit, is still supernatural in its source and impact. It's God working through that person in that specific way.

Did They Stop? The "Cessationism" Debate

Now, this is where things can get a bit debated. You might have heard the term cessationism. This is the belief that certain spiritual gifts, usually the more miraculous ones like prophecy, tongues, and healing, stopped or "ceased" after the first century.

Why do people believe they stopped? The main argument is often that those "sign gifts" were needed to authenticate the apostles and the message of the early church before the New Testament was complete. The thinking goes: once the Bible was written down, those specific gifts weren't necessary anymore.

A key Bible passage they often point to is 1 Corinthians 13:8-10, where Paul says, "Love never ends. As for prophecies, they will pass away; as for tongues, they will cease; as for knowledge, it will pass away". Then he says this happens "when the perfect comes". So, cessationists often interpret "the perfect" as the completed Bible.

But if you keep reading, Paul also says in verse 12: "For now we see in a mirror dimly, but then face to face. Now I know in part that I shall know fully even as I have been fully known". "Face to face" sounds like more than just having the Bible, doesn't it? It sounds like seeing Jesus when He returns!. Many scholars argue that "the perfect" refers to Jesus's second coming and the state of glory when our knowledge will be complete because we'll be with Him. We definitely don't "see face to face" yet; we still "see dimly". So, if "the perfect" hasn't come yet, the argument that the gifts stopped based on this verse seems weaker.

Here's another point: back in 1 Corinthians 14:12, Paul tells believers, "Since you are eager for manifestations of the Spirit, strive to excel in building up the church". The clear purpose of the gifts is to strengthen and grow the church. So, here's the question: Is the church finished being built? Definitely not! There's still so much work to do, people to reach, and believers to encourage. Does it make sense that God would give the early church these essential tools for building, but then take them away before the job was done? It's like trying to build a house, but the builder takes your hammer and saw away halfway through. Why would the Holy Spirit stop equipping the church for its mission? The work didn't end with the book of Acts.

And what about church history? Did these gifts just vanish after the apostles? While the Bible is our final authority, if you look through church history, you do find accounts suggesting these gifts continued. Not always everywhere, perhaps, but often popping up, especially during times of revival or when the gospel was spreading to new places. So, it wasn't like a complete shutdown. The historical evidence suggests maybe not.

Happening Now: The Global Church

Bringing it to today, are these gifts actually happening now? Absolutely. If you look around the world, especially in places like Africa, Asia, and South America, there are literally millions of Christians who report experiencing God's power through healing, prophecy, tongues, and other gifts. It's a massive part of the global church's life! And it's not just hype or emotional highs. While you always need discernment, these experiences are often tied to genuine life change: people turning from sin, finding real faith, and communities being transformed. And crucially, any genuine gift always needs to point back to Jesus. The goal is to glorify Christ, not the person using the gift. If the focus shifts to the person, that's a warning sign.

"What If I Haven't Experienced This Stuff?"

This is such a common and understandable question: "What if I've never experienced any of this? Does that mean something's wrong with me?" The answer goes back to 1 Corinthians 12:11: "The Spirit apportions to each one individually as he wills." "As He wills," not as *we* will. It's His sovereign choice. Not everyone gets every gift or even the same gifts. The key isn't feeling bad if you haven't had a specific experience, but being open, being willing, and saying, "Okay, God, however you want to use me, I'm available". This helps remove that pressure to perform or conjure something up.

Misuse vs. Purpose: Handling Gifts Wisely

Another question: What about gifts like tongues? Aren't they kind of weird or even dangerous if misused? That's a valid concern, and honestly, they *can* be misused. That's why Paul spends so much time in 1 Corinthians 14 giving instructions. He stresses that gifts must be used with love, for building others up, and in an orderly way, especially in church gatherings. Uncontrolled or chaotic use doesn't honor God because, as Paul says, "God is not a God of confusion, but of peace". So, the problem isn't the gift itself, but how it's sometimes practiced without wisdom or love. When used according to biblical guidelines, the goal is always edification and peace, not confusion or drawing attention to oneself.

Can I Ask for Gifts?

Okay, last question for now: What if someone wants to experience these gifts? Like, you've read this, you're hearing about it, and you think, "I want God to use me like that." Is it okay to ask God for spiritual gifts?

Not just okay, it's encouraged! 1 Corinthians 14:1 says, "Pursue love, and earnestly desire the spiritual gifts." Paul even adds, "especially the gift of prophecy," because it directly builds up the church. If your heart is truly motivated by wanting to love people better, serve the church more effectively, and see God glorified, then absolutely ask Him! Ask the Spirit to equip you for His service. He loves to give good gifts.

Your Supernatural Life: A Challenge

So, summing this up, what's the big takeaway for you, listening right now?

1. **You are not powerless.** If you know Jesus, the Holy Spirit lives in you. That's incredible power available.

2. **You're not too young.** Seriously, look through the Bible—God uses young people all the time. Your age isn't a barrier for the Spirit.

3. **It's not too late.** Maybe you feel like you've missed out, or your church doesn't talk about this much, but the same Spirit who moved so powerfully in the book of Acts is here today. He hasn't changed.

A practical step you could take right now: Just start by praying. Simply ask the Holy Spirit, "God, what gifts have You given me? How do You want to use me?" Be open. Look for ways, even small ways, to step out and serve or encourage someone this week. Start small. Be willing.

And always remember to stay rooted in the Bible and let love guide everything you do. You're not just a believer; you're called to be a Spirit-empowered disciple. The same God who moved so powerfully in Acts is absolutely still moving today.

Study Guide 4

SUPERNATURAL YOU: EMBRACING SPIRITUAL GIFTS TODAY

I. Introduction: Demystifying Spiritual Gifts

- Spiritual gifts like prophecy, tongues, and healing can seem confusing or outdated.

- It's easy to assume they were only for the early church or "ultra-spiritual" people.

- However, these gifts are meant for believers today, including you.

II. Foundational Understanding: Purpose and Source

- **Source:** All gifts come from the same Holy Spirit, the same Lord, the same God. God does not use a "cookie cutter" and there's a diversity in how the Spirit works.

- **Purpose:** "To each is given the manifestation of the Spirit *for the common good*".

    o They are not primarily for personal spotlight, but for serving others and building up the whole community of the church.

    o The Holy Spirit wants to empower you to make a real difference, giving your life purpose and power.

- o These gifts are vital for the church to be healthy and grow; they are not optional extras.

III. What Are These Gifts?

(Examples from 1 Corinthians 12, Romans 12, Ephesians 4)

- **Prophecy:** Speaking truth prompted by the Spirit; often encouragement, challenge, or comfort, not just future prediction.

- **Speaking in Tongues:** Speaking in unlearned languages by the Spirit's power.

- **Interpretation of Tongues:** Ability to understand and explain what was said in tongues.

- **Healing:** God restoring health supernaturally.

- **Miracles:** Acts beyond natural explanation.

- **Word of Wisdom/Knowledge:** Spirit-given insight into situations or truths.

- **Discernment of spirits:** Figuring out if something is from God or not.

- **Also includes more "ordinary" gifts:** Teaching, Encouragement, Service, Leadership, Giving, Acts of Mercy.

- **Key Point:** ALL these gifts, whether spectacular or practical, *originate from the Holy Spirit* and are supernatural in source and impact when empowered by Him.

IV. The "Cessationism" Debate: Did Gifts Stop?

- **Cessationism:** The belief that miraculous gifts (prophecy, tongues, healing) "ceased" after the first century, often argued they were only for authenticating apostles or before the New Testament was complete.

- **Counter-Arguments:**

  o **1 Corinthians 13:8-10:** "The perfect" (when gifts pass away) is more likely referring to Jesus's second coming, not the completed Bible ("face to face" with God). We still "see dimly".

  o **1 Corinthians 14:12:** Gifts are for building up the church. The church is still being built, so why would God remove essential tools before the job is done?

  o **Church History:** Accounts suggest these gifts continued, especially during revivals or gospel spread.

  o **Global Church Today:** Millions of Christians worldwide, especially in Africa, Asia, and South America, experience these gifts actively, leading to genuine life change and transformation.

  o **Authenticity:** Genuine gifts always point back to Jesus and glorify Christ, not the person using the gift.

V. Personal Experience and Seeking Gifts

1. "What if I haven't experienced this?"

- o "The Spirit apportion to each one individually as he wills". Not everyone gets every gift or the same gifts; it's His sovereign choice.

- o The key is to be open, willing, and available to God's use.

2. Misuse vs. Purpose

- o Gifts can be misused (e.g., chaotic use of tongues).

- o Paul emphasizes that gifts must be used with love, for building others up, and in an orderly way ("God is not a God of confusion, but of peace").

- o The problem is often poor practice, not the gift itself.

3. Can I Ask for Gifts?

- o Yes, it's encouraged! "Pursue love, and earnestly desire the spiritual gifts" (1 Corinthians 14:1).

- o Especially desire prophecy, as it directly builds up the church.

- o If motivated by love for people and desire to serve, ask God to equip you.

VI. Challenge: Your Supernatural Life

1. **You are not powerless:** The Holy Spirit lives in you, providing incredible power.

2. **You're not too young:** God uses young people; age is not a barrier for the Spirit.

3. **It's not too late:** The same Spirit from the book of Acts is still active today.

4. **Practical Step:** Pray and ask the Holy Spirit, "God, what gifts have You given me? How do You want to use me?". Be open and willing to step out and serve or encourage others.

5. Always stay rooted in the Bible and let love guide everything. You are called to be a **Spirit-empowered disciple.**

Chapter 5

MORE THAN JUST TRYING HARDER: THE FRUIT OF THE HOLY SPIRIT

Y ou've probably had moments where you just wish you could be a better person—more patient, more kind, more in control. Maybe you've told yourself, *"Okay, today I'm going to be calm no matter what."* But then your sibling pushes your buttons, your phone lights up with bad news, or something unexpected throws off your whole day. Suddenly, all that effort feels like it's gone out the window.

That kind of frustration is familiar. You want to grow. You want to be more like the people you admire—calm, kind, steady. But no matter how hard you try, it can feel like you're just pretending, like you're putting on a mask instead of really changing.

Here's the truth: real transformation isn't about trying harder. It's about something deeper—something the Holy Spirit does in us from the inside out. In this chapter, we're going to explore how God produces real growth in our lives—not through willpower, but through His Spirit.

It's Not a Checklist (Thank Goodness!)

Let's get one thing straight right away: what we're talking about here isn't some checklist of virtues you need to achieve through sheer willpower. It's not like a new self-help routine where you just try harder to be a good person. In fact, trying to force these qualities – like deciding to act more loving or gritting your teeth to be patient – actually misses the whole point.

This isn't about just behavior modification, like changing what you do on the outside without changing who you are on the inside. It's about something far more profound: transformation.

Living by the Spirit: A Deep Change

The idea comes from an ancient text, Galatians 5:22-23, which lists nine incredible qualities: love, joy, peace, forbearance (which means patience), kindness, goodness, faithfulness, gentleness, and self-control. These are described as "the fruit of the Spirit." And what's crucial is that these aren't things you manufacture on your own.

Just before this list, the text talks about "walking by the Spirit". This isn't about following a rigid set of rules. It's about living life in step with and being actively led by God's Holy Spirit, who lives inside believers.

When you live connected to God's Spirit, He doesn't just give you tips or motivation. He actually changes you from the inside out. These nine qualities aren't something you have to somehow "make" happen. Instead, they are the evidence, the natural result, that God is at work growing His character in you. It completely flips the script from "I need to do better" to "I need God to work in me".

What Does This "Fruit" Look Like?

When the Spirit grows these qualities in you, they look radically different from our own human attempts. Let's unpack them:

- **Love:** This isn't just liking your friends or feeling warm fuzzies. This is a supernatural ability to love the difficult person – the one who really gets under your skin, maybe even your enemies. It mirrors how Christ loved us unconditionally.

- **Joy:** This isn't just happiness that depends on what's happening, like getting tons of likes on your post or your team winning. That kind of happiness is fleeting. Spirit-given joy is a deep-seated confidence and peace in God that sticks around even when life is genuinely hard or disappointing. It's a deep anchor, underneath your circumstances.

- **Peace:** Instead of being totally consumed by anxiety about the future or stressed about what people think, the Spirit brings a trust in God's control that calms that internal storm. Even when things outside are chaotic, it's an internal quietness.

- **Forbearance (Patience):** When you feel that impulse to snap back at someone, get super frustrated, or just give up on a person or situation, the Spirit gives you the strength to hang in there. It's about extending grace and waiting with hopeful endurance instead of just reacting.

- **Kindness:** This is more than just being superficially nice or giving polite smiles. This is the Spirit opening your eyes to actually see other people's needs and hurts and then prompting you to act with genuine compassion and thoughtfulness. It's proactive.

- **Goodness:** This isn't just about avoiding bad stuff. It's an active desire, stirred up by the Spirit, to actually do what is right and honorable – to align your actions with God's heart for the world around you. It's positively oriented.

- **Faithfulness:** This fruit shows up as loyalty and steadfastness, like sticking with God even when doubts creep in or things get tough. It's also about being dependable and committed in your relationships – being someone people can count on, even when it's inconvenient.

- **Gentleness:** Sometimes this sounds weak, but it's actually power under control. It means having strength and convictions, but expressing them with humility, wisdom, and care for others, avoiding harshness or steamrolling people with your opinions.

- **Self-control:** This is the Spirit empowering you to have mastery over your impulses, your anger, your desires, what you say, what you look at online. So, you're not constantly just ruled by your immediate feelings or cravings. It's freedom from being controlled by those things.

Looking at that whole list unpacked, it feels less like abstract ideas and more like a picture of someone who's truly anchored and secure.

Your Part: Staying Connected Like a Branch

If it's the Spirit doing the work, growing this fruit, does that mean we're just passive? Do you just sit back and wait for patience or joy to magically show up? Not at all!

Think about the powerful analogy Jesus himself used: the vine and the branches (John 15:4-5). A branch connected to a vine doesn't strain and work super hard to make grapes pop out, right? It just stays connected. The grapes grow naturally. They are the result of the branch simply remaining connected to the vine, letting the life of the vine flow through it.

Jesus is the Vine, the source of all life and strength. You are the branch. The Holy Spirit is the power and the life that flows from Jesus into you as you stay connected. You don't produce the fruit by trying harder. The fruit is the natural outcome, the evidence, of staying intimately connected to the Spirit, allowing Him to work in you. It totally shifts the focus from your striving to His indwelling presence and power.

Practically Speaking: How to Stay Connected

So, what does staying connected or "walking by the Spirit" actually look like day-to-day? It breaks down into some really practical, doable things – not complicated, but intentional:

1. **Daily Invitation:** Consciously start your day by inviting the Holy Spirit to lead you. Just acknowledging, "Okay God, I need your power today to navigate stuff, to show your fruit." Talk to Him! Remember, He's a person, not just some vague force. Invite Him into your day.

2. **Feed Your Spirit:** Just like your body needs food to function, your spiritual life needs nourishment. What you consume really matters. Prioritize things like actually spending time reading God's Word, praying, being part of a healthy Christian community, or listening to worship music that connects you. These things feed your connection to the Spirit and give Him room to work.

3. **Get Back Up When You Stumble:** This is so important because you absolutely will stumble! You're not going to nail this perfectly. There will be times you mess up, when your old habits or impulses kind of get the upper hand. But the Spirit's work isn't about shaming you when you mess up. It's about conviction – that gentle nudge that says, "Hey, that wasn't right." This leads to repentance, saying you're sorry, and getting back into relationship. It's not game over when you fail. When you fall, confess it, turn back to God, and let Him continue His shaping work. Get back up.

4. **Stay Connected to the Source:** This reinforces the vine analogy. Prioritizing your actual relationship with Jesus through prayer, worship, reading scripture, and being actively involved with other believers is all essential. The more time and focus you genuinely

give to connecting with Him, the more the Spirit can produce His fruit in you. It flows from that relationship.

Why This Matters For You

This transformation isn't just for Sundays or quiet moments; it touches every single part of your life. Think about it:

- How you handle stress.
- How you respond under pressure.
- How you treat people who are different from you or people who annoy you.
- What kind of presence you have online – your comments, what you share.

It's all impacted by whether you're running on your own fumes or allowing the Spirit to work. As the Spirit grows His fruit in you – that love, joy, peace, patience – people around you, like your friends, family, and even classmates, will notice. They'll see something different in how you handle things, something stable, something genuinely good. And that difference isn't just you trying to be a nicer version of yourself. It's actually God's Spirit working in you. It's about moving beyond just trying to put on a show of good behavior (which is exhausting anyway!) and allowing the Spirit to cultivate genuine, deep-rooted character that actually reflects Jesus to the world.

A Personal Challenge

So, here's a question to consider: Are you actively letting the Holy Spirit lead you?

If you look at that list – love, joy, peace, patience, and all the rest – and you feel a bit discouraged, like, "Man, I don't see much of that in myself," the encouragement here isn't, "Okay, grit your teeth and try harder starting tomorrow!". It's actually simpler, and maybe harder in a way: it's to ask the Spirit to do the work, to surrender those areas to Him. He's the one who grows the fruit. Your part is staying connected like the branch to the vine, cooperating with His leading.

It's a truly liberating perspective, isn't it? Knowing that the power for real change comes from His presence working in you, not just from your own striving.

So, what areas in your life, maybe big ones, maybe small ones, do you need to consciously surrender to Him today? Trust Him to grow His fruit there instead of just trying to force it on your own steam.

Study Guide 5

THE FRUIT OF THE HOLY SPIRIT: TRANSFORMATION WITHIN

I. Core Concept: Real Transformation from Within

- Real transformation isn't about trying harder or willpower. It's not a checklist or behavior modification.

- It's a deep change that the Holy Spirit does in us from the inside out.

- The "fruit of the Spirit" are nine incredible qualities listed in Galatians 5:22-23.

- These qualities are the natural result or evidence that God is at work growing His character in you, shifting focus from "I need to do better" to "I need God to work in me".

II. The Nine Qualities of the Spirit's Fruit

These qualities are radically different from human attempts and are grown by the Spirit:

1. **Love:** Supernatural ability to love difficult people and enemies, mirroring Christ's unconditional love.

2. **Joy:** A deep-seated confidence and peace in God that remains even when life is hard, an anchor beneath circumstances.

3. **Peace:** An internal quietness and trust in God's control that calms internal storms, even amid external chaos.

4. **Forbearance (Patience):** Strength to hang in there, extend grace, and wait with hopeful endurance instead of reacting or giving up.

5. **Kindness:** The Spirit opening your eyes to others' needs and hurts, prompting genuine, proactive compassion and thoughtfulness.

6. **Goodness:** An active, Spirit-stirred desire to do what is right and honorable, aligning actions with God's heart.

7. **Faithfulness:** Loyalty and steadfastness to God even amidst doubts, and being dependable/committed in relationships.

8. **Gentleness:** Power under control, expressing strength and convictions with humility, wisdom, and care, avoiding harshness.

9. **Self-control:** Spirit-empowered mastery over impulses, anger, desires, and what you say or consume online, leading to freedom from being ruled by them.

This list paints a picture of someone truly anchored and secure.

III. Your Part: Staying Connected Like a Branch

- You are **not passive;** fruit doesn't just magically appear.

- **Analogy:** Like a branch connected to a vine, you don't produce fruit by straining; it grows naturally by staying connected.

- **Jesus is the Vine,** the source of life and strength; **you are the branch.**

- The Holy Spirit is the life and power flowing from Jesus into you as you stay connected.

- The fruit is the natural outcome of intimate connection to the Spirit, allowing Him to work.

IV. How to Stay Connected ("Walking by the Spirit")

This involves practical, intentional daily actions:

1. **Daily Invitation:** Consciously start your day by inviting the Holy Spirit to lead and empower you.

2. **Feed Your Spirit:** Prioritize nourishing your spiritual life by reading God's Word, praying, being part of healthy Christian community, and listening to worship music.

3. **Get Back Up When You Stumble:** When you mess up, the Spirit brings gentle conviction, leading to repentance, getting back into relationship, and letting Him continue His shaping work.

4. **Stay Connected to the Source:** Prioritize your relationship with Jesus through prayer, worship, scripture, and involvement with other believers. The more you connect, the more the Spirit can produce fruit.

V. Why This Matters For You

1. This transformation impacts every part of your life, including how you handle stress, respond to pressure, treat others, and interact online.

2. People around you will notice the difference – something stable and genuinely good.

3. It moves you beyond trying to put on a show and allows the Spirit to cultivate genuine, deep-rooted character that reflects Jesus.

VI. Personal Challenge

1. Ask the Holy Spirit to do the work in areas where you feel discouraged or lack fruit, surrendering those areas to Him.

2. Cooperate with His leading by staying connected like the branch to the vine.

3. Trust Him to grow His fruit instead of trying to force it on your own steam.

Chapter 6

WHEN WORDS FAIL:
THE HOLY SPIRIT, YOUR PRAYER PARTNER

Have you ever tried to talk to God, but it feels like you've hit a wall? Like your mind is spinning with school stress or friend drama, or maybe you're just so overwhelmed with sadness or anger that words feel impossible. Or worse, maybe you've messed up so badly that you feel like God's not even interested in hearing from you right now. You want to pour your heart out, but there are just no words, not even a coherent thought for prayer.

It's a super common feeling, isn't it? You're definitely not alone if you feel that way. When youth leaders or adults tell you, "Just pray about it," which is fundamentally good advice, what do you do when you literally feel clueless? Where do you even start?

The Good News: God Knew and Provided Help

The really, really good news is that God knew we'd have moments like this. He knew we wouldn't always be strong or eloquent or even sure of ourselves. He knew life gets messy and confusing. Our weak moments and struggles aren't a surprise to Him. And He already made a way, providing help for exactly these times.

That help comes from someone we might not always connect with our prayer struggles: the Holy Spirit. We often think about Jesus or God the Father, but the Holy Spirit's role in our prayer life, especially when we're struggling, is huge. Understanding this can seriously change everything about how you talk to God.

Your Divine Prayer Partner: Unpacking Romans 8:26

Let's dive into a powerful verse that gets right to the heart of it: Romans chapter 8, verse 26. It says, "In the same way, the Spirit helps us in our weakness. We do not know what we ought to pray for, but the Spirit himself intercedes for us through wordless groans".

- **God Gets You (Even When You're Weak):** The first part, "The Spirit helps us in our weakness," hits hard. It tells us that God is incredibly realistic and compassionate. He knows we won't always have it all together. It's not like you have to pretend you're fine for God to listen. In fact, those moments of weakness are exactly when the Holy Spirit's help is most available and active.

- **It's Okay to Be Clueless:** The verse then says, "We do not know what we ought to pray for". See? The Bible itself admits that sometimes we're clueless in prayer. If you've ever felt lost, unsure what the right thing to pray is, or just totally blank, you're not failing. It's acknowledging a real part of the human experience.

- **Your Divine Prayer Partner:** Which makes the next part even more amazing: "But the Spirit himself intercedes for us". "Intercedes" is a big word. Think of it like this: the Holy Spirit steps in for you, on your behalf. He acts like your divine prayer partner. When you can't find the words, He's like your translator, your helper, right there with you in that messy, silent, confusing space where prayer feels impossible. He is literally praying for you! It's not just you failing alone; you're never alone in it.

Prayer Isn't a Performance

One massive takeaway from this truth is that prayer isn't about having fancy words or sounding super spiritual. It's not about getting everything perfectly phrased. It's fundamentally about connection – your heart reaching out to God's heart. You don't need some kind of script.

Remember, you don't have to perform for God. God cares way more about your honesty and your vulnerability than He does about your vocabulary. Jesus Himself said something similar in Matthew chapter 6, verses 7 and 8: "When you pray, don't babble on like pagans, for they think they will be heard because of their many words. Don't be like them, for your father knows exactly what you need, even before you ask him". So, God already knows your needs. Your job isn't to explain it perfectly. The focus is on the Father's knowing and understanding, not your perfect articulation.

"Wordless Groans": The Spirit Understands Your Unspoken Pain

This brings us to a powerful and comforting part of Romans 8:26: "wordless groans". What does that mean practically? Think about those times when you're just overwhelmed, and your soul hurts, and you literally cannot put words to the feeling because it's too deep or too confusing.

Maybe it's just letting out a huge sigh when everything feels like too much. Or tears start falling, and you don't even know why. Or maybe it's that internal ache where you desperately want to cry out to God, but all you can manage inside is a silent "help," or not even that—just pain.

The Holy Spirit takes that – that deep unspoken emotion, that feeling that's too raw, too complex for your vocabulary. He takes the sigh, the tears, the silent ache, that tangled mess of wordless feeling, that "groaning" the verse talks about, and He communicates it perfectly to God the Father. How? Because He understands the depth of your heart, the root of what you're going through, even when you're completely confused by it yourself. He translates the true core need of your heart directly to God with perfect clarity. It's like having someone who knows you better than you know yourself in that moment speaking for you.

Praying with God's Wisdom: The Spirit Aligns Your Heart with God's Will

Building on this, the Spirit also aligns what's in your heart with God's perfect will. Let's be honest, sometimes we don't know what's actually best for us. We might pray for something that seems good right now from our limited perspective, like praying to ace a test you didn't study for, or for relief from a difficult situation without seeing the bigger picture God might have. We don't always know what we truly need for our growth or for His ultimate good purposes.

So, the Spirit doesn't just filter our prayers or redirect them; He aligns them. He intercedes – He takes our deepest needs, those wordless groans, or sometimes even our misguided requests, and He brings them into alignment with God's perfect knowledge and loving plan. Romans chapter 8, verse 27, which follows verse 26, confirms this: "The Spirit intercedes for God's people in accordance with the will of God".

This is incredible assurance! Even if your attempt at prayer is clumsy, imperfect, or totally confused, because the Holy Spirit is involved, God still hears the real need and works according to His good plan. It's less about your perfect prayer and much more about His perfect intercession and God's perfect loving response. It takes the pressure off us having to "get it right".

Why This Is Different: Beyond Rigid Rituals

This truth really makes Christianity feel different, especially when you compare it to other ways of thinking about prayer. What stands out is the contrast with any system where prayer feels like a rigid ritual or a performance you have to nail. In some ways of thinking, you might feel you absolutely have to use certain words, perform exact actions, or achieve a specific mental state, or else God won't listen or you won't get the desired result. It can feel like you're trying to climb this really tall, precarious ladder to reach God, terrified of slipping up.

But Christianity says something radically different. God doesn't demand you perfectly climb that ladder. Instead, He comes down! He sends a helper, the Holy Spirit, to be right there with you on the ground floor, especially when you feel like you can't even take the first step. You don't have to earn your way to be heard through perfect praying. The Spirit Himself bridges that gap, taking your heart, messy as it is, directly to the Father.

God isn't some distant, demanding boss you have to impress with your spiritual jargon. He's presented as a loving Father who genuinely wants to connect with you. And the Holy Spirit is the one who makes that intimate, relational connection real and accessible, even (and especially) when you're just a wordless mess.

When You Still Feel Nothing: Trusting Beyond Feelings

Okay, real talk for a second. You can hear all this amazing stuff and understand it intellectually, but what if you still sit down to pray and feel nothing? Totally distant, like you don't feel the Spirit helping at all? That's a super real and important question because feelings are powerful, but they aren't always reliable indicators of reality, especially in faith.

It's crucial to remember that our faith journey is ultimately based on the truth of who God is and what He has promised, not primarily on our shifting emotions. The truth is, God is listening, even if you don't feel listened to. The truth is, God is always present, always attentive, even when your feelings are screaming the opposite. And the Holy Spirit's work – His helping, His interceding for you – isn't switched on or off based on how spiritual you feel that day. It doesn't depend on your emotional state at all. His help is a constant reality promised in scripture. He is always working, always interceding according to God's will, always on your side, whether you feel that warmth and connection in the moment or not. That's something solid to hold on to when the feelings aren't there – it's the anchor. His faithfulness isn't dependent on our feelings.

Putting It Into Practice: How to Pray When You Can't

Knowing all this, knowing the Holy Spirit is your helper, can truly change how you approach those moments of feeling blank or lost. It can shift it from frustration or guilt to dependence. Instead of just giving up, you could actually pray about not being able to pray! You could pray something really simple and honest, leaning into the Spirit's help. Maybe something like this:

> "Okay, Holy Spirit, I really don't even know how to pray right now. I feel confused or overwhelmed, or maybe I messed up, and the words just aren't there. I don't know what to say or even what to ask for. But thank you for the truth that you are my helper. Thank you that you understand what's really going on in my heart, even the wordless stuff, and you bring it before the Father. Please help me just trust you right now. Lean into your presence and remember that even when I'm totally speechless, you are still working, still interceding for me. Amen".

That kind of prayer feels completely different, doesn't it? It's not about having the answers, but about trusting the helper. It rests entirely on the truth of who the Spirit is and what He does for you.

Key Takeaways to Remember

Let's boil down the big points to remember about prayer and the Holy Spirit:

- **You don't need perfect words.** Forget performance. Just bring your willing, honest heart to God. Just show up.

- **The Holy Spirit is your personal helper in prayer.** He's actively involved, given specifically to assist you.

- **He understands your heart perfectly, even when you don't.** He gets the confusion, the pain, the "groans," even the wordless stuff.

- **He aligns your prayers, your needs, your heart with God's perfect will.** He makes sure it all works together for ultimate good according to God's plan.

These four truths should absolutely take the pressure off your prayer life. They ground your prayer life in God's grace and the Spirit's power, not your own ability.

Want to Dig Deeper? Explore These Verses

If you want to dig into this more yourself, besides Romans 8:26-27, which is central, check out these scriptures:

- **John 14:26:** Jesus talks about the Spirit teaching us and reminding us of truth, which definitely helps guide our prayers.

- **Galatians 4:6:** This beautiful verse says, "The Spirit enables us to cry out, *Aba*, Father." It speaks to that incredible intimacy the Spirit fosters, allowing you to call God "Daddy".

- **Ephesians 6:18:** This verse urges us to "pray in the Spirit on all occasions with all kinds of prayers and requests." This reinforces His active involvement; it's about praying with His help, relying on His guidance.

Your Challenge

Knowing all this, how will it change your conversations with God this week? Take a moment to really let these truths sink in. Consider these questions for yourself:

1. Have you ever tried to pray and just nothing came out? You didn't know what to say? How did it make you feel in that moment?

2. Do you ever find yourself feeling like God won't really listen unless you get your prayer just right, like you need certain words or a certain tone? Be honest with yourself on that one.

3. Thinking about the Holy Spirit as your active helper, the one who understands your wordless groans and aligns your heart with God's will – how does knowing that truth potentially change how you view prayer, especially in those tough, speechless moments?

Let these thoughts challenge and encourage you. This new perspective on the Holy Spirit's help in prayer can give you some real hope and transform those moments of frustration into opportunities for deeper connection with God.

WHEN WORDS FAIL: THE HOLY SPIRIT, YOUR PRAYER PARTNER

I. The Common Struggle of Prayer

- Many feel clueless or find words impossible when trying to talk to God, especially when stressed, sad, angry, or feeling they've "messed up".

- God anticipated these moments of weakness and provided help.

II. God's Provision: The Holy Spirit, Your Helper

- The Holy Spirit's role in prayer is "huge" and can "seriously change everything" about how you talk to God.

- Romans 8:26-27 is central to understanding this role:

    o "The Spirit helps us in our weakness". God is realistic and compassionate, and the Spirit's help is most active in these moments.

    o "We do not know what we ought to pray for". It's okay to be clueless or blank; you are not failing.

    o "The Spirit himself intercedes for us". He acts as your "divine prayer partner," stepping in on your behalf, like a translator or helper, literally praying for you.

- o "Through wordless groans". The Spirit takes deep, unspoken emotions—sighs, tears, internal aches—and communicates them perfectly to God the Father, understanding the root of your heart even when you're confused.

- o "The Spirit intercedes for God's people in accordance with the will of God". He aligns your deepest needs, even misguided requests, with God's perfect knowledge and loving plan, taking the pressure off you to "get it right".

III. Key Principles of Prayer

- **Prayer isn't a performance:** It's about connection—your heart reaching God's heart. God cares more about your honesty and vulnerability than your vocabulary. He already knows what you need.

- **Beyond Rigid Rituals:** Christianity is different; God doesn't demand you perfectly "climb a ladder". Instead, He comes down by sending the Holy Spirit to bridge the gap and connect your messy heart directly to the Father. God is a loving Father who wants to connect, not a demanding boss.

IV. Trusting Beyond Feelings

- Even if you feel nothing when you pray, remember that faith is based on God's truth and promises, not shifting emotions. The Holy Spirit's help is a constant reality promised in scripture, not dependent on your emotional state.

V. Practical Application: How to Pray When You Can't

- When words fail, pray about not being able to pray.

- An example prayer involves being honest, thanking the Spirit for being your helper, trusting Him to understand and intercede, and leaning into His presence. This rests on trusting the helper, not on your own answers.

VI. Key Takeaways to Remember

- You don't need perfect words; just bring your willing, honest heart.

- The Holy Spirit is your personal helper in prayer, actively involved.

- He understands your heart perfectly, even the "wordless groans."

- He aligns your prayers with God's perfect will.

- These truths take the pressure off your prayer life, grounding it in God's grace and the Spirit's power.

VII. Verses for Deeper Exploration

- **Romans 8:26-27**: Central to the Spirit's intercession.

- **John 14:26**: Spirit teaches and reminds, guiding prayer.

- **Galatians 4:6**: Spirit enables intimacy ("Aba, Father").

- **Ephesians 6:18**: Praying "in the Spirit" reinforces reliance on His guidance.

VIII. Personal Challenge

- Reflect on moments you couldn't pray and how you felt.

- Consider if you've felt pressured to "get your prayer just right."

- Think how knowing the Holy Spirit as your active helper changes your view of prayer, especially in tough, speechless moments.

Chapter 7

YOUR PERSONAL GUIDE: FINDING GOD'S PLAN FOR YOUR LIFE

ave you ever found yourself staring at the ceiling at 2 AM, wondering, "What am I supposed to do with my life?" Or maybe, "How can I possibly know what God actually wants for me?" And the big one: "What if I make a huge mistake and mess up my whole future?" If any of those questions hit home, you're definitely not alone. These worries are super common, and they're exactly what we're going to explore.

The amazing news is this: You are not left alone to figure life out. God hasn't just given you a map for your life; He's given you a personal guide. That guide is the Holy Spirit. Jesus knew His followers would face confusion, uncertainty, and tough choices, so He promised they wouldn't have to walk through any of it blindly. The Holy Spirit is presented as your guide, your teacher, and your counselor, actively helping you step into the unique path God has for you. He's not just some abstract concept; He's here to empower you to live out God's purpose day by day.

To understand how He guides, it's helpful to remember who the Holy Spirit is. The Bible teaches that He is fully God, a person with a will and emotions, not just some mysterious force. And here's the profound part: if you follow Jesus, the Holy Spirit actually lives inside you (1 Corinthians 6:19). This means you have internal guidance, not just external rules. He also empowers you with strength and character to live more like Jesus, giving you what the Bible calls "the fruit of the Spirit" (Acts 1:8, Galatians

5:22-23). This personal, indwelling guide is here to help you discover and live out God's unique purpose for your life.

So, how does this incredible guide actually work? How does the Holy Spirit practically lead you? There are four key ways:

1. He Guides Through Truth (God's Word)

Remember that promise from Jesus? John 16:13 says, "When He, the Spirit of truth, comes, He will guide you into all the truth". The Holy Spirit's main job is always to point you back to Jesus, who is the Truth, and to what He has revealed. This means something absolutely foundational: the Holy Spirit will never lead you to do something that contradicts the Bible, ever.

So, if you're wrestling with a decision, your first filter should always be: Does this line up with Scripture? Is it consistent with what God has already clearly said? This also means God's will isn't some hidden code you have to crack. The Spirit reveals it mainly through the clear teachings of the Bible. He makes God's Word feel alive and relevant specifically to you in your situation, applying that truth directly to your life right now.

2. He Whispers to Your Conscience (That Inner Voice)

You know that inner voice, that sense of conviction you sometimes feel when you're thinking about a choice? That's often how the Holy Spirit works! Romans 8:14 says, "For those who are led by the Spirit of God are the children of God". This is about those internal nudges – a prompting towards something good and right, or perhaps a warning away from something harmful.

Of course, not every random thought is from the Spirit. We have our own thoughts, and lots of other influences. But when that inner prompting lines up with what the Bible teaches and brings a sense of peace or a gentle conviction that just feels right, that's often the Spirit's voice. Because He literally lives inside believers, His voice, while often quiet, is real and distinct. It's more like a gentle leading, not usually a loud command. Think of it like tuning into a specific radio frequency – you have to listen for it.

3. He Uses Your Gifts and Passions

This is really encouraging! God specifically wired you a certain way, on purpose. He made you *you* for a reason. The Holy Spirit doesn't just empower you generally; He gives specific spiritual gifts (like wisdom, faith, teaching, or leadership, mentioned in 1 Corinthians 12:4-11) to build up others.

But it's not just about those supernatural spiritual gifts. He also stirs up your natural talents and passions – the things you're naturally good at, or the things you care deeply about. He takes those and aligns them with God's purposes, with His kingdom work. So, finding your purpose feels personal because it is personal. God isn't asking you to suddenly become someone completely different. Instead, it's about letting the Spirit redeem or transform your natural abilities and passions for something bigger. For example, if you love art, maybe the Spirit directs you to use that for creative ministry. If you're a great listener, perhaps He uses that gift in counseling or being a supportive friend. Passionate about tech? Maybe that becomes your avenue for sharing truth online. The Spirit takes your unique makeup and uses you for something with eternal meaning.

4. He Leads Through Community

You are not meant to figure this all out in isolation. Sometimes the Spirit speaks through other people in your life – trusted mentors, parents, leaders in your church, or close friends who are also seeking God. They might say something that confirms what you've been feeling or praying about, or offer a different perspective you hadn't considered (but one that still lines up with Scripture!).

The powerful insight here is that faith isn't just a private "me and God" thing; it's deeply communal. The Bible shows over and over how God works through His people to speak into individual lives. So, actively seeking counsel from trusted believers is actually a way of inviting the Spirit to use others to help guide you.

What About When You Mess Up?

Now, let's talk about that giant fear we mentioned at the start, the one that can be paralyzing: "What if I make the wrong choice? What if I miss God's plan entirely?" That fear is so real, isn't it? Like God has this one perfect, narrow path, and if you step off it even slightly, you're doomed.

Here's a powerful truth: God's will isn't as fragile as you might think. This doesn't mean choices don't matter, of course they do. But it means God isn't easily thwarted. He's presented as a redeemer, someone who can take even our mistakes, our wrong turns, and work with them to get us back on track if our heart is truly set on following Him. Proverbs 3:5-6 captures this perfectly: "Trust in the Lord with all your heart and lean not on your own understanding. In all your ways, submit to him and he will make your paths straight".

It's less about a rigid plan and more about ongoing trust. Purpose is presented as a journey, not a fixed destination, guided step by step by the Spirit. This takes so much pressure off, doesn't it?

How to Actively Engage with His Guidance

So, how do you actively engage with this guidance? What are the practical steps you can take today?

1. **Pray for Guidance:** It sounds simple, but just ask! Ask the Holy Spirit before you make decisions, big or small, to show you the way.

2. **Read Scripture Daily:** His leading always aligns with His truth, so spending time in the Bible is like getting familiar with His voice, His character, and His priorities.

3. **Listen in Silence:** This is about intentionally creating quiet space. Tune out the noise – maybe just five minutes in the morning or before bed. Be still, try to quiet your own racing thoughts, and be attentive to that inner nudge or sense of peace.

4. **Talk to Wise Believers:** Don't go it alone. Actively seek out mentors, pastors, or older Christians you respect and trust. Share what you're wrestling with, ask for their perspective, and ask them to pray with you.

5. **Pay Attention to Peace:** While not the only indicator, when you are in step with the Spirit's leading, there's often an underlying sense of clarity, calm, or peace that comes with it, even if the decision itself is hard.

These steps are tangible ways to connect with your guide. You can see how this works in real life when you look at stories in the Bible:

- **Philip and the Ethiopian Man (Acts 8:26-40):** The Spirit gave Philip a very specific, unusual instruction: "Go stand next to that chariot." Philip obeyed, and it led to an amazing conversation where the Ethiopian understood the scriptures and came to faith in Jesus. That's a direct, specific nudge!

- **Paul's Missionary Journeys (Acts 16:6-10):** Paul and his team wanted to go preach in one area, but the text says the Holy Spirit prevented them – closing that door. Then, Paul had a vision of a man from Macedonia calling for help, which redirected them entirely, opening a new door for the gospel in Europe. The Spirit sometimes says "no" to one path to open another.

- **Jesus Himself (Luke 4:1):** Right after His baptism, Jesus was led by the Spirit into the wilderness to be tempted. Even Jesus relied on and followed the Spirit's guidance for His life and ministry!

These stories show the variety of His guidance: direct instruction, a closed door, or even a leading into a tough season – but it's always purposeful guidance.

Your Unique Purpose, Guided by God

Bringing it all together, the main message is clear: You truly don't have to figure out your life and purpose all by yourself. The Holy Spirit isn't some distant force. He's walking with you, speaking to you in these different ways we've discussed, and strengthening you from the inside out. He's helping you live the specific life God designed you for – not just to survive it, but to truly thrive in your unique purpose. It's not about finding some hidden map; it's about walking daily with the One who knows the way.

A Personal Challenge: Stepping into Your Story

As you think about all of this, consider these questions:

- What's a specific decision you're facing right now where you really feel you need the Holy Spirit's guidance?

- Looking back, have you ever felt what you think might have been one of those inner nudges from God before? What happened, and what did that feel like?

- How can you actively create more quiet space in your day or week just to be still and practice listening for the Holy Spirit's voice?

- Thinking about your own unique makeup: What gifts or passions do you have that maybe God is calling you to use for His purposes?

These aren't tests, just invitations to think and engage personally.

Finally, here's a simple prayer you can make your own:

> *"Holy Spirit, I want to know and live out the purpose you have for my life. Help me hear your voice, trust your direction, and follow Jesus step by step. Even when I'm unsure, remind me that you are with me and that you will guide me into all truth, shape my passions, decisions, and future for God's glory. Amen".*

This prayer really captures it: asking for help, acknowledging the uncertainty, but ultimately trusting the Guide. You are equipped. You have a personal guide, the Holy Spirit, who is actively helping you navigate life, make choices, and step into the purpose God created specifically for you. Keep exploring what it means to be led by the Spirit.

Study Guide 7

GUIDED BY THE SPIRIT: FINDING GOD'S PLAN FOR YOUR LIFE

I. Introduction: The Holy Spirit as Your Personal Guide

- It's common to wonder "What am I supposed to do with my life?" or fear making mistakes.

- You are not alone in figuring life out; God has given you a personal guide: the Holy Spirit.

- Jesus promised the Holy Spirit would be a guide, teacher, and counselor to help you step into God's unique path and empower you daily.

II. Who is the Holy Spirit?

- The Holy Spirit is fully God, a person with will and emotions.

- If you follow Jesus, the Holy Spirit lives inside you (1 Corinthians 6:19), providing internal guidance, not just external rules.

- He empowers you with strength and character, producing "the fruit of the Spirit" (Galatians 5:22-23).

III. Four Key Ways the Holy Spirit Guides You

1. Through Truth (God's Word):

- The Holy Spirit never contradicts the Bible; He is the "Spirit of truth" (John 16:13).

- He makes God's Word alive and relevant to your specific situation.

- Your first filter for any decision should be: "Does this line up with Scripture?"

2. Whispers to Your Conscience (That Inner Voice):

- This is often an internal nudge, a prompting toward what is right or a warning away from harm.

- While not every thought is from the Spirit, His voice is real and distinct for believers, often a gentle leading that brings a sense of peace or conviction when it aligns with the Bible.

3. Uses Your Gifts and Passions:

- God specifically wired you. The Holy Spirit gives spiritual gifts (e.g., wisdom, faith, teaching, leadership from 1 Corinthians 12:4-11) to build up others.

- He also stirs up your natural talents and passions, aligning them with God's purposes (e.g., using art for ministry, listening for counseling, tech for sharing truth online).

- Finding your purpose is personal, as the Spirit redeems and transforms your natural abilities for something bigger.

4. Leads Through Community:

- o You are not meant to figure this out alone; the Spirit often speaks through trusted mentors, parents, church leaders, or close friends who are also seeking God.

- o They might confirm your feelings, offer new perspectives (consistent with Scripture), or provide counsel.

- o Faith is communal, and seeking counsel from trusted believers is a way to invite the Spirit's guidance.

IV. What About When You Mess Up?

- The fear of missing God's plan is common, but God's will isn't fragile.

- God is a redeemer who can take even your mistakes and wrong turns and work with them to get you back on track if your heart is truly set on following Him.

- It's more about ongoing trust ("Trust in the Lord with all your heart… in all your ways submit to him and he will make your paths straight" - Proverbs 3:5-6) than a rigid, unchangeable path. Purpose is a journey, guided step by step.

V. How to Actively Engage with His Guidance (Practical Steps)

1. **Pray for Guidance:** Simply ask the Holy Spirit to show you the way before decisions.

2. **Read Scripture Daily:** Spend time in the Bible to get familiar with His voice, character, and priorities, as His leading always aligns with His truth.

3. **Listen in Silence:** Intentionally create quiet space to tune out noise and be attentive to inner nudges or a sense of peace.

4. **Talk to Wise Believers:** Seek counsel from trusted mentors, pastors, or older Christians; share your struggles and ask for prayer.

5. **Pay Attention to Peace:** An underlying sense of clarity, calm, or peace often accompanies being in step with the Spirit's leading.

VI. Biblical Examples of Guidance

*   **Philip and the Ethiopian Man (Acts 8:26-40):** The Spirit gave Philip a specific instruction to approach a chariot, leading to conversion.

*   **Paul's Missionary Journeys (Acts 16:6-10):** The Holy Spirit prevented Paul from going to one area, then redirected him through a vision to Macedonia, opening a new door for the gospel.

*   **Jesus Himself (Luke 4:1):** Even Jesus was "led by the Spirit into the wilderness," showing His reliance on the Spirit's guidance.

*   These examples show the Spirit's guidance can be direct instruction, closed doors, or even leading into tough seasons, but it is always purposeful.

VII. Your Unique Purpose, Guided by God

- You don't have to figure out life by yourself; the Holy Spirit is walking with you, speaking in these ways, and strengthening you.

- He helps you live the specific life God designed for you to thrive in your unique purpose, not just survive. It's about walking daily with the One who knows the way.

- **Personal Challenge:** Consider a decision you're facing, reflect on past inner nudges, commit to creating quiet space, and think about how God might use your unique gifts and passions.

- Pray for help to hear His voice, trust His direction, and follow Jesus, confident that He will guide you and shape your future for God's glory.

Epilogue

YOU WERE NEVER MEANT TO WALK ALONE

As you close the final chapter of this book, I hope you're walking away not just with more information—but with a deeper awareness that you are not alone. Ever.

The Holy Spirit is not an optional part of the Christian life. He is essential. He is God. He is with you right now. The same Spirit who hovered over the waters at creation, who filled prophets and apostles with courage and clarity, who raised Jesus from the dead—now dwells in you.

Let that truth shape you.

The goal was never just to understand Him better. It's to know Him personally. To listen. To respond. To walk with Him. To allow His fruit to grow in you. To let His gifts flow through you. To live not by your own strength, but by His.

This journey isn't about having all the answers—it's about making space for the Spirit to lead, comfort, convict, and empower. It's about saying "yes" to the daily whisper of God in your heart.

So go forward with courage. You are filled with the Spirit of the Living God. He is your Helper, your Guide, your Teacher, your Friend.

And He's not forgotten you.

He's been waiting for you to remember Him.

Now walk with Him—and never look back.